ASSEMBLIES FOR SCHOOL
AND CHILDREN'S CHURCH

ASSEMBLIES
FOR SCHOOL
AND
CHILDREN'S CHURCH

by

THE REVEREND R. H. LLOYD

Chaplain of the Dragon School

Oxford

THE RELIGIOUS EDUCATION PRESS LTD.

A Member of the Pergamon Group

A. Wheaton and Company (Educational Publishers), Hennock Road, Exeter EX2 8RP.

Pergamon of Canada Ltd., P.O. Box 9600, Don Mills, Ontario M3C 2T9, Canada.

Pergamon Press (Aust.) Pty Ltd 19a Boundary Street, Rushcutters Bay, N.S.W. 2011, Australia

First edition 1974

Reprinted 1975

To—Hazel, Catherine and Simon.

Printed in Great Britain by A. Wheaton & Co., Exeter
ISBN 0 08 017776 X

CONTENTS

PREFACE

Most people when drawing up an act of worship for school assembly choose a theme and then proceed to build around it. I have followed this traditional pattern in the compilation of the following services, bearing in mind the age range for which the services were arranged.

Before the passage of scripture is read, I think that it is extremely important to plant the *idea* of the theme in the mind of the child through the use of a story. The story, if it has come across, will shed light on the teaching contained in the scripture passage, and the child gets the point.

Constructing a service for the 9–13 year old age group, especially when the school worships as a family, has one particular difficulty. If the language is pitched too low, the average child feels that he or she is being talked down to, and this is resented. Again, if the language is pitched above them, the object of the operation is defeated.

I have always felt that a good story can—if properly told—rivet the attention and prepare the mind for a short act of worship, and leave the child with the satisfied feeling that he has understood.

The prayers and stories chosen for this collection are those which I have found to be effective and meaningful to this particular age group, both in parish and school setting. Each Assembly includes a choice of two hymns which can be found in most of the current school hymn books.

I cannot claim that any part of this work is my own. It is the product of listening to and reading the works of those men and women who seem to have the knack of getting across to children. It would be impossible for me to acknowledge all my sources because I have long since forgotten where or when I heard a particular story. So I declare my indebtedness to anyone who may recognise a story and, in particular, to The Venerable H. C. Williams, Archdeacon of Gower, from whom many of these stories originated.

R. H. Lloyd,
The Dragon School,
Oxford.

A PRAYER

The School

Almighty God, in whom we move and live and have our being, make this school as a field which the Lord hath blessed, that whatsoever things are true, pure, lovely and of good report, may here forever flourish and abound. Preserve in it an unblemished name, enlarge it with a wider usefulness, and exalt it in the love and reverence of all its members as an instrument of thy glory, for the sake of Jesus Christ our Lord.

Henry Hayman.

1.

GOD IN EVERYTHING

Aim

This world is God's world and He is to be found everywhere.

Story

One of the most famous of the smaller art galleries in the world is to be found in the ancient Belgian town of Bruges. The guide book tells you that it is near the church of Notre Dame. In fact it is most difficult to discover because who would think of looking for an art gallery in a hospital? But that is exactly where it is. In a room, tucked away, adjacent to the wards of the sick and dying. There you will find the world-renowned *Casket of St. Ursula* almost within sound of the metallic clatter of oxygen cylinders and food trolleys; there you will see the priceless paintings of *The Marriage of St. Catherine, The Entombment* and *The Epiphany*. All these, where the sick and weary come and go.

One would not expect to find works of art in such a setting. One might suppose that renowned pictures of this calibre would be hung in a purpose-built hall, separate from the ways of everyday life. But there it is, such beauty, almost hidden, in the middle of life at the heart of Bruges.

This is a fine parable of the love and beauty of God.

We are not only to look for his love and beauty in some cloistered monastery or soaring cathedral or quiet country church, where, of course, He most surely is. We can also seek and find Him amongst the bustle of daily business, where men and women work, where families are brought up, where children are educated; in the common by-ways of life.

READING:

Genesis 28, 10–19. 'Truly the Lord is in this place, and I did not know it.'

PRAYER:

We thank thee, O Father, for the sun that warms us, and the air that

1

gives us life; for all the beauty of the earth, in field and hedgerow, brook and covert, woods and hills; for the changing seasons, each in its order beautiful; for happy homes and cheerful faces; for health and vigour of body and mind; for the food that makes us strong; for freedom and just laws; for the lives and examples of the good and brave of every age and every race; and for the life on earth of Jesus— our example, who came to show us how to live.

(*Hymns and Prayers for Dragons*).

The Lord's Prayer.

HYMNS: *All things bright and beautiful.*
For the beauty of the earth.

2.

UNASHAMED

Aim

No one need be ashamed to be a follower of Jesus Christ.

Story

It wasn't until John was about twelve years old that he really became self-conscious about his mother's hands. Although she was in every other way a beautiful woman, her hands were terribly scarred and twisted.

John's father was the first to notice that something was troubling him. He was also the first to notice that John, who had once brought his friends home to play, now no longer did so.

When the opportunity presented itself, John's father took him for a walk into the garden.

'I have noticed,' he said, 'that you no longer bring your friends here like you used to.'

John made no reply.

'I was just wondering why,' continued his father. 'Is there any reason?'

'No!' came the answer.

'I see,' said the father, 'but I couldn't help wondering whether it might not be because of mother's hands. I mean, it might be that you do not want your friends to see them.'

John flushed to the roots of his hair, but remained silent.

'Perhaps you would like to know how your mother came to have such hands,' said his father, 'because when I married her they were very lovely.'

John still made no comment. So his father continued.

'It all happened one day when you were just able to toddle about. You and your mother were in the garden. She turned her back for a moment and you headed for the house. The back door was open and you made for the fire place, pushed away the guard, and stood too close to the flames. Your clothes caught fire and the flames soon began to lick their way around you. You screamed, mother rushed in, and because there was nothing else available and the flames were growing, she smothered the fire with her own hands. She saved you but sacrificed her hands in doing so.'

John just looked ahead and said nothing. His father left him with his own thoughts.

Soon, however, John once again began bringing his friends around to the house for a game or to tea. He always made a point of asking his friends very discreetly to note his mother's hands.

'You see,' he would say, 'she burnt them because she loved me so much.'

READING:

St. John 20, 24–29. 'Unless I see the mark of nails on his hand . . . I will not believe.'

PRAYER:

O Lord Jesus Christ, who hast called us to be thy servants, grant that we may not be ashamed to confess Christ crucified, but may fight manfully under thy banner against sin, the world and the devil, and continue thy faithful soldiers and servants unto our lives' end.

(The Book of Common Prayer—adapted).

The Lord's Prayer.

HYMNS: *Stand up; stand up for Jesus.*
Fight the good fight with all thy might.

3.

THE DAILY ROUND THE COMMON TASK

Aim

To show that it is one of the facts of life that the day's work can produce the greatest things.

Story

For years Johann Sebastian Bach was a teacher and organist at St. Thomas's School in Leipzig.

He was paid a salary of £125 per annum and was required to train the boys' choir and play the organ at Sunday services, weddings and funerals. He was also expected to produce new musical compositions every Sunday.

These musical works were never published during his lifetime. They were simply written, sung and then piled into a vestry cupboard and there left to grow old and dusty and eventually forgotten. Such priceless music as *Sheep may safely graze, Jesu, joy of man's desiring, O sacred head now wounded.*

Bach's music, in every probability, would have been lost had it not been for a young Jew named Mendelssohn who just happened to find the manuscript of the *St. Matthew Passion* in his music teacher's home.

Mendelssohn was brilliant enough to recognise that whoever the composer was, he must have been a genius.

A massive search was immediately organised and a vast amount of Bach's music was discovered. Cantatas, Chorales, Concertos, Overtures, pieces for the organ and piano.

But it was also discovered that a large quantity of Bach's works were irretrievably lost because for some eighty years generations of choir boys had been using the manuscripts from the cupboard for wrapping around their sandwiches!

Be that as it may, Bach did not compose with any thought of fame. He regarded himself as a man with a job to do, like everyone else, and got on with it to the best of his ability. And in so doing gained immortality as a musician.

READING: St. Matthew 13, 44.

PRAYER:

O Lord our God, in whose hands is the issue of all things, who requirest from thy stewards not success, but faithfulness: Give us

4

such faith in thee, and in thy sure purposes, that we measure not our lives by what we have done, or failed to do, but by our obedience to thy will; through Jesus Christ our Lord.

(Daily Prayer)

The Lord's Prayer.

HYMNS: *New every morning is the love.*
Teach me, my God and King.

4.

THE SIGN OF THE FISH

Aim

To pose the question: Are we the sort of people to whom others can come for help?

Story

From time to time as the Christian Church began to spread across the Roman Empire it was fiercely persecuted and thousands of Christian men and women were savagely tortured and put to death. It became unsafe for anyone to admit that he was a Christian because it would lead to certain arrest. In order to recognise one-another Christians used secret signs, and one of these was the sign of the fish, which could be easily scratched on a wall or marked out in the dust.

Not so long ago, in a suburb of Oxford called Headington, a number of Christians got together to discuss ways and means of helping those who lived in the community who, from time to time, might need help. An old person who had to visit a distant hospital. A mother of little children who would appreciate an afternoon baby-sitter occasionally. Someone suddenly faced with an emergency.

A list was drawn up of people who were prepared to help in various ways and a secretary was appointed to handle all requests. These helpers called their venture 'The Fish Scheme'. Little silver badges were made and members were encouraged to wear this ancient Christian symbol in their lapels.

Soon the people of Headington learnt about The Fish Scheme and many have, and many still continue, to benefit from it.

Later a further development took place. All old people were encouraged to keep a black cardboard fish in their houses, so that in times of need they could hang the fish in their windows. Milkmen, postmen and neighbours were asked to keep a sharp look out so that help could be bought to anyone displaying this distress signal.

Today the scheme has spread far and wide and thousands of people are benefiting from it.

READING:

St. John 13, 3–9 and 12–17. Jesus washes the feet of his disciples.

PRAYER:

O Lord teach us to sacrifice our comforts to others, and our likings for the sake of doing good. Make us kindly in thought, gentle in word, generous in deed. Teach us that it is better to give than to receive, better to forget ourselves than to put ourselves forward; better to minister than be ministered unto. And unto thee the God of love, be all glory and praise, both now and for evermore.

(Henry Alford—1810–1871).

The Lord's Prayer.

HYMNS: *When I needed a neighbour were you there?*
Kumbaya, my Lord, kumbaya.

5.

HAPPINESS

Aim

To show that God has put happiness within our reach. We should not make the mistake of thinking that it is on the horizon.

Story

There is a legend of an angel who came one evening to the brink of a river and asked the boatman to ferry him across. When they reached the other side, the angel gave the boatman what appeared to be a handful of shavings in payment for his services. The boatman was so disappointed and disgusted with his reward that he threw the shavings into the river.

6

Next morning as he ferried another traveller across, he noticed one or two of the shavings lying in the bottom of the boat, and on examining them closely, realised that they were not shavings at all but gold parings. Gold! And he had thrown them away.

READING: Job 28 (selected), 1, 2, 12–15, 18, 20, 21, 23, 26–28.

PRAYER:

O God, whose word is better than gold, and thy counsels than precious stones: Grant us wisdom to seek the true riches, to know thee and possess thee, and to be known and possessed of thee; through Jesus Christ our Lord.

(Daily Prayer).

The Lord's Prayer.

HYMNS: *Our blest Redeemer, ere he breathed.*
O Thou not made with hands.

6.

THE SECOND CHANCE

Aim

We need never hesitate to go to God for pardon. He is always ready to give us another chance.

Story

Jeremiah, the prophet of God, had been wondering for some time why God had not given him a message for the people. Then, one day, God said to him, 'Go down to the potter's house, and there I will tell you what I have to say.'

The prophet obeyed God's word and turned into the cool, damp atmosphere of the potter's workshop, a welcome change from the dry, torrid heat of the street.

Inside, Jeremiah watched, fascinated by the skill of the potter as he spun the wheel with his feet and skilfully shaped a wet lump of clay into a graceful pot with his sensitive hands.

Perhaps it may have been that Jeremiah's shadow falling across the wheel disturbed the potter's concentration, for his hand slipped a

7

fraction and the pot, which was nearing completion, was spoilt. Jeremiah no doubt apologised for having distracted the potter, and then noticed that the potter did not throw the spoilt lump of clay away. He merely squeezed it together and started again. The potter had given the clay a second chance.

Immediately Jeremiah saw the message God had given him. God had decided to give the people of Jerusalem a second chance.

READING: St. Luke 15, 11–24. The parable of the Prodigal Son.

PRAYER:
Almighty God, our heavenly Father, who of thy great mercy hast promised forgiveness of sins to all them that with hearty repentance and true faith turn unto thee, have mercy upon us; pardon and deliver us from all our sins; confirm and strengthen us in all goodness, and bring us to everlasting life; through Jesus Christ our Lord.
                    (*The Book of Common Prayer—adapted*).
The Lord's Prayer.

HYMNS: *There's a wideness in God's mercy.*
Jesus, where'er thy people meet.

7.

INFLUENCE

Aim

To show that the right influence at the right moment can have tremendous results.

Story

Much of the sugar we find on our breakfast-tables is home-produced In the late autumn the sugar-beet is harvested from the countryside and taken to the eighteen sugar-beet factories we have in this country.

The roots are washed, sliced and crushed. The juice extracted from the pulp is then filtered and strained and eventually crystalised into the sugar we recognise.

There is one process which is particularly interesting.

When the juice is completely purified, it is emptied into a vast pan and heated. A man watches the temperature rising and at the exact moment he empties a tiny spoonful of powdered sugar into the boiling liquid. This has the immediate effect of turning some two tons of juice into sugar crystals, which is then cooled and packed into cartons ready for distribution.

READING: St. Matthew 13, 33.

PRAYER:
Almighty God, use us we pray thee in thy service; make us sanctuaries of thy presence and channels of thy power. Grant that we may shed abroad thy influence in our lives, that when our fellow men look at us they may see the reflection of Jesus Christ.

The Lord's Prayer.

HYMNS: *Take my life, and let it be.*
Ye servants of God, your Master proclaim.

8.

DIFFICULTIES

Aim

To show that difficulties are part and parcel of life, that they should be tackled and not avoided. A life without difficulties is a life without achievement and colour.

Story

A gardener one day noticed a chrysalis attached to the wall of his tool shed. He kept a close watch on it, and one day observed that the chrysalis had begun to open. While the gardener stood and watched, the split gradually grew longer and wider until eventually the head of the emerging butterfly appeared. For the next hour the man stood transfixed as he observed the tremendous struggle put up by the insect as it fought to free itself from its leathery prison. At last, with a mighty push and a twist, the butterfly was free, and slowly unfolded its wings to dry in the sun. As he watched, he saw the wings take on the most lovely and beautiful colours; and then the butterfly flew away.

A year later the same man came across another chrysalis which was beginning to split and he decided to help matters on a little. Fetching a razor blade, he very gently and carefully slit the chrysalis open, allowing the butterfly to emerge with complete ease. The creature spread its wings to dry and flew away. But there was one big difference between the butterflies. The second had no colour in its wings. The gardener recognised that a life without struggle can be a life without colour.

READING:

2 Corinthians 11, 23–31. The more difficulties Paul encountered the greater he grew as Christ's ambassador.

Genesis 37, 39, 40, 41. A condensed account of Joseph's life can show how a spoilt son achieved greatness through difficulties.

PRAYER:

> Teach us, good Lord
> to serve thee as thou deservest;
> to give and not to count the cost;
> to fight and not to heed the wounds;
> to toil and not to seek for rest;
> to labour and not to ask for any reward,
> Save that of knowing that we do Thy will.
> *(Ignatius Loyola).*

The Lord's Prayer.

HYMNS: *Father hear the prayer we offer.*
Fight the good fight.

9.

GOD'S HANDS

Aim

To show that the only hands God has in this world are our hands.

Story

During the war an old church in Germany was bombed. Everything was destroyed except for a life-sized statue of Jesus which stood against the east wall; it survived unscathed except for its hands which had been completely shattered.

10

The people who worshipped in the church very carefully removed the statue, wrapped it in straw, placed it in a large wooden box and hid it in a deep cellar.

When the war was over, the church was re-built and the statue of Jesus was restored to its original place.

Some years later a very able sculptor happened to visit the church and was extremely interested to notice that the figure of Jesus had no hands. He went in search of the priest and after a short conversation offered to carve new hands for the statue free of charge. The priest thanked the man for his offer and said that he would put the matter before the members of the church.

A meeting was duly held and the matter was discussed at great length. Finally a vote was taken. The church members decided not to accept the sculptor's offer, 'Because,' they said 'the statue reminds us, each time we go to pray in church, that Jesus has no hands in this world except our hands.'

READINGS:

Acts 9, 32–42. Peter heals Aeneas and Tabitha, carrying on the healing ministry of Jesus. Also cf. St. Luke 8, 43–56. The raising of Jairus' daughter.

Acts 9, 10–17. God asks Ananias to go and lay his hands on the head of the newly converted Saul, in Damascus.

PRAYER:

> Christ has no body now
> on earth but yours,
> No hands but yours,
> No feet but yours;
> Yours are the eyes
> through which is to look out
> Christ's compassion to the World,
> Yours are the feet
> with which he is
> to go about doing good;
> Yours are the hands
> with which he is
> to bless us now.
>   (*St. Teresa of Avila*).

The Lord's Prayer.

HYMN: *Forth in thy name, O Lord, I go*
        Take my life, and let it be.

11

10.

WE MEET JESUS DAILY

Aim

To show that whenever we help a fellow man we are in fact helping Jesus.

Story

Crispin was a shoemaker who lived in Soissons seventeen hundred years ago. He was not only a skilled craftsman, he was also extremely kind. No poor person ever left his shop without having been given a hot bowl of soup, a cloak or a pair of sturdy shoes. His door was always open to the needy.

One night in deep winter as he drifted into sleep, he had a dream. In the dream he saw an angel, who told him that as a reward for his kindness, Jesus would pay him a visit on the following day.

The next morning Crispin awoke early and set about tidying his house; he built up a roaring fire and put on a fresh pot of stew. He dressed himself in his best clothes and waited to receive his guest.

Mid-way through the morning there came a knock on the door. 'That must be Jesus!' he thought. Full of excitement he flung open the door only to find a little boy, blue with cold, shivering on the step.

'Please may I come inside?' pleaded the boy. 'I'm so dreadfully cold.

Crispin looked at him and clearly wanted to ask him to step inside, but thinking that Jesus might arrive at any moment, he gave the boy a coin and directed him to an inn lower down the road.

'I'm sorry,' he said, 'but I cannot attend to you now, I'm expecting a visitor.' And, closing the door on the little chap, Crispin went back to his fire-side and waited.

A little after mid-day, it started to snow, and Crispin threw a few more logs on to the fire. And then there came another knock. 'This must be him' he thought and rushed to answer the door. But, when he opened it, he saw a frail woman clothed in rags holding a baby.

'Please may I come inside?' she asked, 'My baby is frozen through and I cannot keep him warm.'

Crispin gazed at her for a moment and was on the point of ushering her into the warmth of his room, when he remembered that he was expecting Jesus.

'I'm sorry,' he replied "but it isn't convenient at the moment, here is a coin, go down to the inn at the bottom of the road and they will supply you with hot food and let you warm yourself at their fire in

12

exchange for the coin.' The woman accepted the money and slowly walked away. Late in the afternoon, as the light was beginning to fade, there came yet another knock. Crispin's heart leapt, 'This must be him, it is getting so late!'

He opened the door, but was deeply disappointed to find an old beggar-man standing in the snow, pleading to be allowed inside. 'I'm so cold,' he cried 'if I have to remain outside in this snow tonight I shall die. I haven't eaten for two days.' Crispin felt terribly torn between letting the old man in, and the thought that Jesus must surely be on the point of arriving. 'Look!' said Crispin, 'Much as I would love to share my home with you this night, it is rather difficult. You see, I am expecting someone important and it is just not convenient. Here, take this coin, and go down to the inn at the bottom of the road, they will give you a hot meal and shelter.' The old man took the coin, murmured his thanks and turned into the gloom.

Time passed and night fell. Crispin realised that there would be no more callers. Deeply disappointed, he went up to bed and fell asleep.

Again he dreamt and again the angel appeared. Crispin looked at the angel reproachfully and said, 'I thought you told me last night that Jesus was going to call on me today.' 'But he did,' replied the angel very solemnly. 'He called on you three times, but on each occasion you turned him away. Whom do you think the little boy, the baby in the woman's arms and the beggar-man were?'

READING:

St. Matthew 25, 31–40. 'Inasmuch as you have done it unto one of the least of these my brethren, you have done it unto me.'

PRAYER:

O Lord who hast promised in thy Gospel that whatever is done unto the least of thy brethren, thou wilt receive as done unto thee; give us grace, we humbly beseech thee, to be ever willing and ready to minister, as you have given us ability, to the needs of our fellow creatures, and to spread the blessings of thy kingdom over all the world, to thy praise and glory. *Amen.*

The Lord's Prayer.

HYMN: *When I needed a neighbour were you there?*
Lord of all hopefulness, Lord of all joy.

13

11.

SPREADING THE WORD

Aim

We should never be shy of declaring our faith in Jesus Christ.

Story

A new abbot was appointed to a monastery and immediately set about tightening up the discipline. He noticed that there were some monks who did not take their turn to preach the sermon on Sundays. The abbot drew up a new list and every monk noticed that his name appeared opposite a particular Sunday.

Brother John, whose main job in the monastery was washing up the dishes and cleaning pots and pans, was filled with horror when he saw his name on the list. He went to the abbot and explained that he had been excused by the previous abbot from preaching because he was no good at it, and begged to have his name removed. The abbot refused, 'If I excuse you, Brother John,' he said, 'others will want to be excused also, and I cannot have that!'

Time passed and the dreaded Sunday came round. All the other monks were filled with mirth at the thought of Brother John preaching and they could scarcely take their eyes off him all through the service. Eventually the moment came to make his lonely way between the rows of monks to the pulpit. When he arrived and looked down on the sea of upturned faces, his nerve almost broke. His tongue seemed dry and there was an awful silence as everyone waited for him to begin.

After what seemed an age, he managed to ask in a voice which did not sound at all like his own—'Do you know what I am going to say?'

'No!' came the reply from the congregation.

'Neither do I,' croaked Brother John, and fled out of the chapel into an adjoining room.

He was followed by the abbot who very sternly declared, 'That wasn't good enough, Brother John, you will have to try again next Sunday.'

The next Sunday arrived and Brother John once again, with thumping heart, got into the pulpit. Taking a deep breath and licking his dry lips, he asked the same question, 'Do you know what I am going to say?'

'Yes,' they all replied.

'Well then,' said Brother John, 'there is no need for me to tell you!' Again, he fled from the chapel, closely followed by the abbot.

'Look here,' said the abbot, 'I simply will not accept this sort of behaviour. You shall not get away with it. Next Sunday you will preach again; and I shall keep at you until you give us a proper sermon.'

On the third Sunday the monks could hardly suppress their smiles as Brother John slowly made his way to the pulpit, feeling very downhearted. Again, he looked down on the rows of expectant faces and experienced that awful blankness that comes over some people when they have to get up to speak. The only thing he could think of was the same question he had asked on the two former occasions. So he asked it.

'Do you know what I am going to say?' he whispered. Half the monks replied 'No!', the other half replied 'Yes!'

'Well then,' said Brother John brightening up for the first time in months, 'let those of you who know tell those of you who do not know!' And then, very deliberately, he walked out of the chapel and waited.

Ten minutes passed before the abbot appeared. Much to Brother John's surprise the abbot smiled, put his arm around Brother John's shoulders and said: 'What a wonderful message! That was the best sermon I have heard in years. "Let those who know tell those who do not know'."

READING:

2 Timothy 1, 6–10. Paul urges his young friend Timothy to speak up in the name of Jesus.

St. Matthew 28, 16–20. Jesus' final command to his disciples—'Go and teach all men about me.'

PRAYER:

O Lord Jesus Christ,
Teach my mind to think of you;
teach my lips to speak of you;
teach my heart to love you;
teach my hands to serve you.
Amen.

The Lord's Prayer.

HYMNS: *Stand up! Stand up! for Jesus*
Immortal love for ever full.

12.

MISTAKES

Aim

To show that God forgives and that we should not allow our mistakes to mar our lives.

Story

Do you know how to recognise a genuine Persian carpet? Well I'll tell you. Look for the mistake in the pattern. There must be one somewhere.

The Muslim believes that only God (Allah) can create perfection, and if he, the carpet maker, created a carpet with a perfect pattern, he would be trying to be equal with God, and this would be a sin. Consequently the Persian carpet-maker always includes a deliberate mistake in the pattern, but then, with infinite care, blends the mistake into various patterns so that it becomes extremely difficult to spot.

None of us can live a perfect life. Sooner or later mistakes will be made. Jesus, however, assures us that God is always ready to forgive and pardon us. And it is important to remember that having obtained God's pardon, we should not allow that mistake to haunt us; it must not be allowed to mar our lives. To let this happen is to doubt God's word. Like the Persian carpet-maker, we should blend the mistakes into the over-all pattern of our lives, and benefit from them; using them as signposts to avoid temptations when they next appear.

READINGS:

St. Matthew 18, 21–35. 'Lord, how often am I to forgive my brother if he goes on wronging me? As many as seven times?' Jesus replied, 'I do not say seven times; I say seventy times seven.'
St. Matthew 6, 12. 'Forgive us the wrong we have done, as we have forgiven those who have wronged'.

PRAYER:

Lord, for thy tender mercies' sake, lay not our sins to our charge, but forgive us all that is past; and give us strength to amend our lives, to turn away from sin and turn towards goodness, that we may walk with a perfect heart before Thee, now and evermore. *Amen.*
The Lord's Prayer.

HYMNS: *The God of love my shepherd is.*
The Lord's my shepherd, I'll not want.

13.

GOD'S INSTRUMENTS

Aim

To show that God depends on you and me to bring goodness into the world.

Story

At the turn of this century parts of the Scottish Highlands were even more remote and inaccessible than they are today. Many a crofter's cottage stood miles away from the nearest road, isolated by large tracts of moorland.

A brilliant London surgeon, born in Scotland, loved to return each autumn for a fortnight's holiday in the Highland glens, and always stayed at a cosy but isolated inn.

During one of these holidays, very late at night, after everyone had gone to bed, the great knocker on the front door was hammered frantically, waking all the occupants. The landlord lit his lamp and went down to open the door. There, standing on the step, he saw a crofter he knew, white and breathless. The crofter clutched the landlord's arm and gasped 'Is the London doctor here? My daughter has been taken desperately ill and it may be too late to fetch my local doctor.'

The surgeon was called to the door and listened to the crofter's appeal. He immediately returned to his room, dressed, and set off into the darkness with the crofter. After many miles of tramping along a muddy track, they eventually reached the man's cottage and entered the little girl's bedroom. Expertly the surgeon examined the child; then, rising slowly, he whispered, 'Her condition is critical. If I had my instruments, I could save her life. As it is, there is nothing I can do. I am helpless. My instruments are back in London.' And so, the little girl died.

Even the most able doctor is helpless to do anything if he hasn't got his clinical instruments with him.

So it is with God. There is an awful lot he can see needs doing in this world of ours, but unless you and I are prepared to become His instruments, there is nothing even He can do.

READINGS:

Acts 3, 1–16. God uses Peter to heal a cripple.
Exodus 3, 1–12. God calls Moses to be his representative in Egypt.
Or the following ancient legend:

17

'When Jesus ascended into heaven after his work on earth was finished, the Archangel Gabriel met him. Gabriel was a little worried about the future: "Master," he asked, "What arrangements have you made for carrying on your work below?" "I have chosen twelve men," Jesus answered. Gabriel was horrified. "Twelve men to carry the Gospel to the whole world! What if they should fail?" he asked. The reply of Jesus was firm and confident: "I have made no other provision".'

PRAYER:

> Lord, make us instruments of your peace.
> Where there is hatred, let us sow love;
> Where there is injury, pardon;
> Where there is discord, union;
> Where there is doubt, faith;
> Where there is despair, hope;
> Where there is darkness, light;
> Where there is sadness, joy.
>
> *St. Francis of Assisi* (1181–1266).

The Lord's Prayer.

HYMNS: *God be in my head.*
Rise up, O men of God!

14.

GOD REVEALS HIMSELF IN JESUS

Aim

To show how God grappled with the problem of disclosing his nature to man.

Story

Did you know that a radio signal transmitted from Cape Kennedy takes only 1·3 seconds to reach the moon? A distance of 250,000 miles! Or to put it in another way, a radio signal travels at the speed of 186,000 miles per second. Our sun and its planets belong to a galaxy made up of millions and millions of stars. If we were able to travel in a space-ship as fast as a radio signal, it would take us 100,000 years to cross our galaxy! Astronomers tell us that our galaxy is only one of countless millions of other galaxies in the Universe. The distances involved are so staggering that our minds cannot grasp them. And behind all this is what created everything—GOD.

Man has always tried to imagine what this Creator must be like and many great thinkers have attempted to put their thoughts into writing. One of these men was St. Augustine of Hippo a great scholar who lived about fifteen hundred years ago.

Whilst pondering on the subject, he chanced to be walking along the sea shore when he noticed a little boy busily filling his bucket with water, trotting back up the beach and emptying it into a small hole that he had dug in the sand. St. Augustine watched the boy repeating this many times and then, full of curiosity, he asked the child what the object of the exercise was.

'I'm trying to empty the sea into that hole,' replied the boy.

St. Augustine smiled, and then, lifting the child on to his shoulders, began to explain what a vast thing the Mediterranean sea was, and, therefore, how impossible his task.

He gently put the boy down and continued on his way. As he walked he thought about the advice he had just given, and began to realise that his attempt to describe GOD was even more impossible than what the child had been trying to do.

God, however, had already solved the problem, very simply. He had come upon earth in the person of Jesus Christ. All we have to do, if we want to understand God's nature, is to study the teaching and life of Jesus; because Jesus himself said, 'He who has seen me, has seen the Father.'

READINGS:
St. Luke, 1, 26–36. The birth of Christ foretold.
Psalm 8. 'What is man that thou art mindful of him: and the son of man that thou visitest him.'

PRAYER:
O God, whom the pure in heart alone can see:
Grant that we may truly seek thee; and seeking, find thee;
and finding, grow in knowledge of thee;
through Jesus Christ our Lord. *Amen.*

The Lord's Prayer.

HYMNS: *The people that in darkness sat.*
Christ is the Lord of the smallest atom.

15.

PERSEVERANCE

Aim

To elaborate on the truth contained in the following sentence of Sir Francis Drake (1540–1596): 'There must be a beginning of any great matter, but the continuing unto the end until it be thoroughly finished yields the true glory.'

Story

One of the most attractive creatures found in rock pools at the sea-side is the starfish. You may be surprised to know that its favourite food is the oyster, which is exceedingly difficult to open. How then does the starfish manage to perform this difficult feat? First it attaches one of its feet to the top-side of the oyster, and then attaches another to the under-side of the oyster. Having done this, the starfish begins to exert a very gentle pull. The oyster, aware of this attempt to open it, immediately applies all the power of its hinge muscle to keep itself securely shut. The starfish is not deterred; it just keeps on pulling very, very gently, hour after hour. Eventually the oyster has to give in. It cannot keep up such a mighty effort indefinitely; the hinge muscle relaxes and the shell opens and of course the starfish gets its reward.

READING:
Nehemiah 2, 17–end, 3 & 4. (carefully selected).
Jerusalem had been destroyed by Nebuchadnezzar and the Jews carried into captivity. Many years later they were allowed to return, but grew very despondent when confronted by such ruin. Nehemiah, a high ranking Jew in the court of Persia, returns and in the face of indifference, deceit, and outright opposition, sets about rebuilding the Walls of Jerusalem.

PRAYER:
When a job is hard, Lord, help us to persevere until it is completed. When the competition is stiff, encourage us not to give up halfway. Teach us, in everything, to live our lives for Him who persevered until the end, and won our salvation, Jesus Christ, our Lord. *Amen*

The Lord's Prayer.

HYMNS: *Who would true valour see.*
Ride on! ride on in majesty!

16.

VITAL DECISIONS

Aim

To show the importance of cultivating the right kind of friendships and making the right kind of decisions.

Story

Leonardo da Vinci was a famous Italian painter and scholar who lived about five hundred years ago. One of his better known paintings is *The Last Supper*, which he painted on a wall in the convent of Santa Maria delle Grazie.

There is a story that Leonardo painted another picture of the Last Supper which has been lost. In order to make the characters appear life like, Leonardo asked various people to sit as models. When he came across a person who was strong and forceful, he asked him to sit as the model for St. Peter. When he met a man who was gentle and determined, he asked him to sit as a model for St. John. And so on.

Eventually he had only two more models to find. Someone to depict Jesus and someone to depict Judas Iscariot.

One evening at a party he met a young nobleman who had the very face Leonardo was seeking to depict Jesus. Leonardo asked him whether he would sit for him. He explained that he was looking for a particular kind of face that was Christ-like. The young nobleman very graciously accepted the invitation.

Now he was left to find the last face, a face for Judas the traitor. Leonardo knew what he wanted, he wanted a face which looked blatantly evil, twisted and cunning. But search as he would, he just could not find the right face.

Twenty years passed, and the painting remained unfinished.

Then, early one morning, Leonardo happened to be walking through a terrible slum in Florence, when he stumbled over a drunken wretch lying in the gutter. The drunk turned toward Leonardo and cursed him. Leonardo was on the point of walking on, when he paused and looked again at the man's face. This was it! After all these years of waiting, his patience had been rewarded. Leonardo bowed to the wretch lying in front of him and apologised, and at the same time offered him a gold coin. 'If you would like more of those,' he said, 'come to my studio this afternoon. Anyone will direct you. My name is Leonardo da Vinci.'

The drunk arrived, and Leonardo explained why he had been asked to the studio. 'I would like you to sit as the model for Judas Iscariot,' he said, 'your face exactly matches the picture I have of Judas in my mind.'

The man was seated to Leonardo's satisfaction and the great artist began to paint. After a while, Leonardo became conscious of the fact that the man was softly sobbing. He laid down his brushes and said:

'What troubles you? Surely you ought to be happy at the thought of earning some gold so easily.'

The man looked up, and Leonardo could not help but think that this face was the ugliest and most evil he had ever seen.

'Don't you recognise me?' cried the man. 'I'm the person who sat as the model for Jesus Christ twenty years ago.'

READING:

St. Mark 10, 17–22. The story of the rich young ruler who declined the invitation of Jesus. Had he accepted, he might have become as well known as Peter, James or John.

PRAYER:

O Lord, give us clean hands, clean words, and clean thoughts. Help us to stand for the hard right against the easy wrong. Save us from habits that harm. Teach us to work as hard and play as fair in thy sight alone as if all the world saw. Forgive us when we are unkind, and help us to forgive those who are unkind to us. Keep us ready to help others, though at cost to ourselves. Send us chances to do a little good every day, and to grow more like Christ.

(William De Witt Hyde).

The Lord's Prayer.

HYMNS: *Take up thy cross, the Saviour said.*
O Jesus I have promised.

17.

COMMON SENSE

Aim

To show that common sense is a virtue we can all develop.

Story

In the tenth chapter of the first Book of Kings the writer describes

22

the visit of the Queen of Sheba to the court of King Solomon. She was impressed and amazed by the splendour and magnificence of all that she saw.

Before she returned home, it is said that she submitted a request to the King.

'I have heard much about your wisdom, your majesty,' she said. 'May I now be given the privilege of experiencing an example of that wisdom for myself?'

King Solomon smiled and asked her to make her request a little more clear.

'I have in my kingdom,' she related, 'a man who is an extremely skilled artist. He can make artificial flowers that are so life-like, provided they are not handled or smelt, no one can tell them from the real thing. If I placed such a bunch of artificial flowers alongside a bunch of real flowers, could you tell me which is the real bunch?'

King Solomon realised that he could not decline the challenge without damaging his reputation, so he agreed to her request.

The queen signalled to one of her servants who brought in two bouquets of flowers, one real and the other artificial. The servant carefully placed them on a table and retired.

Solomon drew near and looked. He moved around and examined each flower in each bunch closely, he peered at the stems and leaves hoping for one small clue, but he did not find one. The artist had done his job well. The king had to face the fact that unaided he would just have to guess and hope for the best.

Then a thought came to him. He pretended that he felt like some fresh air and asked the guard to open the windows.

What he hoped for happened. A bee flew in from the gardens, and after buzzing around the room a few times, approached the flowers, and of course landed on the real ones. The bee knew which was which!

'There!' exclaimed the king triumphantly, pointing at the bunch on which the bee was busily working. 'That is the bouquet of real flowers.'

READING:

St. Matthew 22, 15–22. A question is put to Jesus by the Pharisees. If he answers 'No', he will be guilty of treason against Rome. If he answers 'Yes', he will disgrace himself in the sight of his followers.

PRAYER:

God be in my head,
And in my understanding;

23

God be in my eyes,
And in my looking;
God be in my mouth,
And in my speaking;
God be in my heart,
And in my thinking;
God be at mine end,
And at my departing.

Fifteenth Century.

The Lord's Prayer.

HYMNS: *Immortal, invisible, God only wise.*
Through all the changing scenes of life.

18.

PEOPLE AREN'T ALWAYS WHAT THEY SEEM

Aim

To show that we have to know a great deal about a person and a great deal about human nature before we can assess somebody.

Story

Two boys lay in a small hospital ward, both were critically ill and could not be moved. There was one small window near the inner bed. Neither boy could do anything except talk. So the one near the window day after day recounted what he could see going on in the world outside, to help take the other lad's mind off his pain and predicament. He described the trees, the flowers, the birds, the clouds and all sorts of people as they went by on their business.

The fellow in the far bed listened day by day, month by month, and though he appreciated all that he heard, he envied the little boy who was next to the window because he enjoyed such a marvellous view. Again and again, he asked for the beds to be changed round, but nothing was ever done about it.

One day the little lad next to the window had to be moved to another hospital for further treatment, and the fellow who had so envied the view was moved over to the window. When he looked out he saw a

24

blank wall and a couple of dust-bins; there was no view at all. The other little lad had imagined it all for the benefit of his friend.

READING:

1 Kings 3, 16–28. '. . . "Give the living baby to the first woman; do not kill it. She is its mother".'

PRAYER:

O Holy Spirit of love, quicken our imaginations that we may feel more deeply the needs of our fellows; and as we put ourselves in their places give us hearts of self-forgetting compassion which will move us to give from that which thou hast given us, and be good neighbours to our fellow men both near and far; for the sake of him who taught us that it is more blessed to give than to receive, even Jesus Christ our Lord. *Amen.*

(George Appleton).

The Lord's Prayer.

HYMNS: *Our blest Redeemer, ere he breathed.*
Lord of all hopefulness, Lord of all joy.

19.

CHANGE

Aim

To show that when we seek to change things we must be careful not to destroy that which is good.

Story

A housewife asked advice from a neighbour on how to remove a stain from a white table cloth. The neighbour recommended nitric acid for the purpose.

The housewife succeeded in getting rid of the stain all right, but also got rid of the table cloth!

READING: St. Matthew 9, 16, 17.

PRAYER: O God, give us,
>Serenity to accept what cannot be changed;
>Courage to change what should be changed;
>And wisdom to distinguish the one from the other;
>Through Jesus Christ our Lord.

>>>>>(*Reinhold Niebuhr*).

The Lord's Prayer.

HYMNS: *Through all the changing scenes of life.*
O God, our help in ages past.

20.

FAITH

Aim

To show that faith is deeper than belief.

Story

The most daring of tight-rope walkers in history must be the Frenchman, Blondin. He was so fearless that he had a thin wire-rope stretched across the Niagara Falls and there performed the most incredible acts ever beheld on the tight-rope. Just one slip and he would have plunged to his death.

On his first walk across he used a balancing rod. Then, to every one's amazement, he returned across the Falls wheeling a wheelbarrow. The vast crowd cheering him loudly. But Blondin had not finished; his assistant climbed into the wheelbarrow, and Blondin began the return journey with his passenger. Every spectator held his breath. Just one slip! One misjudgement and certain death awaited both performers. After what seemed an age, Blondin and his passenger reached the safety of the other bank. The crowd screamed with relief and appreciation. One fellow with a very loud voice kept shouting, 'Do it again! Do it again!' Blondin turned to him and said, 'Do you believe I can do it, Sir?' 'Yes, of course, I believe,' replied the spectator, 'I've just seen you do it.' 'Then,' replied Blondin, 'will you climb into my wheelbarrow and let me wheel you across?' But the man declined.

Certainly the spectator believed in Blondin, but he didn't have faith in him.

READING:
A paraphrased version of Daniel, chapter 6. Daniel's faith in God is absolute and it brings him safely through.

PRAYER:
Lord, increase our faith. Grant us to know in daily life something more of the faith that pleases thee; the faith that removes mountains; the faith that overcomes the world; the faith that works through love; the faith that makes all things possible. So may we prove more fully thine own faithfulness and receive the blessedness which thou hast promised to those who trust in thee; through Jesus Christ our Lord. *Amen.*   (*Frank Colquhoun*).

The Lord's Prayer.

HYMNS: *O for a faith that will not shrink.*
Put thou thy trust in God.

21.

PRAYER

Aim

To show that God always listens to our prayers, and answers them. At times he has to say 'No', because what we may be asking for would harm us. No father would give his three-year-old child a razor blade to play with! Usually, however, our prayers are answered so wonderfully, that we do not realise that our requests are being attended to.

Story

Two thousand years ago on a mountain in Judaea, three trees happened to be growing together. One was an elm tree, another a beech tree and the third was an oak.

Sometimes they would sway in the breeze and converse.

'What would you like to be?' the oak would ask, bending towards the beech tree.

'Oh I would like to be made into a cradle one day, and be at the centre of loving attention,' came the reply.

'And what would you like to be?' the oak asked the elm.

'I'd like to be made into a sign-post,' the elm would reply. 'To point people in the right direction.'

The elm and beech would then bend toward the oak and ask what it wanted to be.

'I'll tell you, ' the oak would sigh. 'I would love to be made into a yacht and skim across the sea to all sorts of beautiful places.'

One day when they were fully grown, men came with axes and cut them down. The trees were sawn into planks and stored away to season properly.

The months passed when a man came into the timber-yard and bought the beech-wood in order to build a stable.

'But I don't want to be a stable,' moaned the beech, 'I want to be a cradle.'

A few years later, a young woman called Mary gave birth to her son in that stable, and her infant child was gently laid to rest in the manger. No cradle has ever held so precious a child.

Later two fishermen visited the timber-yard wishing to buy oak planks to build a fishing boat.

'I don't want to be a smelly fishing boat!' cried the oak tree, 'I want to be a yacht.'

The fishing boat became the platform from which Jesus one day preached to a large crowd. No yacht has ever served such an exalted purpose.

Then one day, there marched into the timber-yard a number of Roman soldiers. The centurion in charge summoned the owner and said:

'I want some elm planks for making a cross. Do you have any for sale?'

The poor elm felt a terrible shiver running through its length.

'I don't want to be made into a cross on which criminals are put to death,' it sobbed. 'I want to be a sign-post.'

The elm planks were hammered together into a cross, and on that cross Jesus was crucified.

Although the elm didn't realise it at the time, its wish had come wonderfully true. The cross has become the most important sign-post in history, directing men and women to heaven.

28

22.

GIVING

Aim

To show that when we learn to give, we learn to live.

Story

When we look at a map of Palestine we see that there are two small inland seas; the Sea of Galilee and the Dead Sea. A closer look at the map will show us that the two seas are linked by the River Jordan.

The Jordan flows out of the northern hills, enters the upper end of Galilee, flows out at the lower end, proceeds down the Jordan valley and ends up in the Dead Sea. Yet the surprising thing is that, athough these two seas are supplied with the same water, they are completely different in nature.

Around the Sea of Galilee there are towns and villages in abundance. There are farms and trees. Birds nest on its shores, fish abound in its waters. It looks alive. It feels alive. It is alive.

The Dead Sea on the other hand has no villages or towns on its coast-line. There are no pastures, there are no trees. No birds nest on its shores, there are no fish in its waters. It looks dead. It feels dead. It is dead.

Why this great difference?

Another look at the map will provide us with the answer.

The Sea of Galilee is alive because it has an outflow, it passes the water on as swiftly as it receives it. The Dead Sea is dead because it has no outlet. It keeps all the water it receives.

29

READING: 2 Corinthians 9, 6–11. 'God loves a cheerful giver.'

PRAYER:

O Lord Jesus Christ, who hast taught us that it is more blessed to give than to receive, and that to whom much is given much shall be required: Pour into our hearts the spirit of thine own abundant generosity, and make us ready and eager to share with others what we ourselves have so richly and freely received. *Amen.*

The Lord's Prayer.

HYMNS: *O Lord of heaven, and earth, and sea.*
Come down, O love divine.

23.

ALMIGHTY GOD OUR HEAVENLY FATHER

Aim

To show that when we approach our God, we not only approach him as a figure of majesty and awe, but as a person who has invited us to call him father.

Story

When a Roman Emperor achieved a victory in battle, he was given a triumphal entry on his return to Rome. He was preceded by a long column made up of prisoners, hostages, slaves and wagons laden with all manner of loot, and behind him marched his legions.

On one of these occasions, the people of Rome turned out to gaze at the procession and to cheer the Emperor. Suddenly out of the crowd darted the figure of a young boy, heading straight for the Emperor's chariot. Quickly, a centurion stepped from his position and grabbed the boy within yards of the chariot.

'What do you think you are doing?' growled the centurion, 'Don't you realise that that is the Emperor?'

'Let me go!' gasped the boy, kicking and struggling to break the centurion's grip. 'He may be your Emperor, but he is my father.'

30

READING:
St. Luke 11, 1–4. 'When you pray say, Father, thy name be hallowed.'

PRAYER:
Almighty God, whose glory the heavens reveal, the earth thy power, and the sea thy might; and yet for the love of man didst take upon thyself the form of man. Grant that we may always approach thee with lowly reverence and adoring love. *Amen.*

The Lord's Prayer.

HYMNS: *Eternal Ruler of the ceaseless round.*
Holy, holy, holy, Lord God Almighty.

24.

JUDGING OTHERS

Aim

When we assess people we must always be careful to look at their good points as well as the bad.

Story

A teacher took a large sheet of white paper which had a black spot in the middle of it, and he pinned it on to the wall in front of the class.

Turning to the pupils he asked, 'What can you see?'

Up shot every hand. Each person in the class said that they could see a black spot.

'That's very odd,' observed the teacher, 'can't any one of you see the large sheet of white paper?'

*   *   *

There is a story told about Jesus and his disciples which further illustrates this point. Jesus and his disciples were walking into a village when they saw a dead dog lying in the gutter.

'What an ugly brute!' said one of the disciples.

'Look at its filthy coat!' said another.

'What an evil expression it has!' said a third.

'Yes indeed.' said Jesus, 'but have you noticed what lovely teeth it has?'

St. Matthew 7, 1–5. 'Pass no judgement and you will not be judged.'

PRAYER:
Save us, O Lord, from the critical mind that can only find fault and takes for granted the goodness in others. Help us to recognise loveliness and beauty wherever it may be, and see in others a reflection of thy beauty and truth. *Amen.*

The Lord's Prayer.

HYMNS: *Blest are the pure in heart.*
Breathe on me, Breath of God.

25.

PAIN

Aim

To show that suffering is not necessarily negative in its influence, it produces beauty and frequently deepens character.

Story

From very early times up to the present day the pearl has always been prized for its beauty. Kings and queens have decorated their crowns and sceptres with them, and beautiful women seek to add to their loveliness by wearing them as necklaces.

It comes as a surprise, therefore, to learn that this object of beauty is the product of pain. An oyster will only produce a pearl when its survival is threatened.

Whenever a foreign body or harmful organism penetrates an oyster and sets up an irritation, the oyster immediately produces a substance called nacre which seals off the affected area by completely surrounding it. As time passes, more and more nacre is added, and slowly forms into a pearl.

When we cut ourselves, a scar is formed to close the wound, so that harmful bacteria can be shut out and prevented from entering. In a sense, the pearl is the oyster's scar. It is the product of pain.

St. John 20, 24–28. Jesus offered Thomas a pearl of great price; complete assurance that he, Jesus, had risen from the dead. He did this by showing Thomas the wounds in his hands, feet and side.

PRAYER:

Jesus, Friend of the friendless,
Helper of the poor,
Healer of the sick,
Whose life was spent in doing good,
Let us follow in Thy footsteps.
Make us loving in all our words,
And in all our deeds;
Make us strong to do right,
Gentle with the weak,
And kind to all who are in sorrow:
That we may be like Thee,
Our Lord and Master. *Amen.*

The Lord's Prayer.

HYMNS: *The head that once was crowned with thorns.*
The Lord's my Shepherd, I'll not want.

26.

SETTING AN EXAMPLE

Aim

We all have an influence for good or bad over our fellow men.

Story

A very valuable race-horse developed a limp in its front right leg. The owner called out the veterinary surgeon who examined the leg thoroughly from top to bottom, but nothing could be found to account for the condition. To make absolutely sure, the vet fetched his mobile X-ray machine and X-rayed the leg, but the photographic plates showed that everything was in order. The owner still was not satisfied and asked for a second opinion. Another vet was called in, but he too could find no cause for the lameness. Naturally the owner was very distressed at having a first-class horse which he dare not race for fear of causing further damage to the leg.

The days went by, but the horse still limped as badly as ever. They tried massaging the leg and even covered it with a special bandage, but there was no improvement.

One morning, after the owner had been down to get the latest report on the horse, one of the junior stable boys approached him.

'Excuse me, sir!' he said, politely touching his cap, 'May I make a suggestion?'

'Certainly my boy,' sighed the owner, 'I am ready to listen to anything that could help.'

'Why don't you try changing the horse's groom?' asked the stable boy.

'What has changing the groom got to do with a lame leg?' asked the owner raising his eyebrows quizzically.

'Well, sir,' came the reply, 'the groom walks with a very pronounced limp. And I was thinking that since the horse is led to its water and exercise by this groom, the horse is just imitating the groom.'

'It sounds absurd,' said the owner, stroking his chin, 'but anything is worth a try.'

The groom was changed, and sure enough, the limp gradually disappeared.

READING:

Acts 7, 54–60. The death of Stephen may well have influenced the mind of Saul of Tarsus and prepared him for his conversion on the Damascus Road.

PRAYER:

O God our Father, who in the life of thy son Jesus didst give to men the perfect example of thy love, accept and strengthen, we pray thee, the lives of those here who would follow him. Make us strong in will, brave in action, honest in faith: that by thy power our lives may show forth among men the beauty of his life, who is our brother and Lord, Jesus Christ. *Amen.*

The Lord's Prayer.

HYMNS: *Now praise we great and famous men.*
O Jesus, I have promised.

34

27.

SELF DISCIPLINE

Aim

When we have learnt to discipline ourselves we can face any crisis without wavering.

Story

In 79 A.D. the volcano Mount Vesuvius erupted and, in a matter of hours, completely buried the cities of Pompeii and Herculaneum beneath a layer of volcanic ash and mud-lava. This covering had the effect of preserving the cities to such an extent that when archaeologists began to excavate on the sites recently they found eggs, fish and fruit on a dining-room table remarkably preserved.

When the disaster occurred most of the inhabitants managed to get away to a place of safety, but for one reason and another many did not. One of the bodies discovered by the archaeologists was that of a Roman soldier who had been standing on sentry duty. It would seem that his garrison commander had failed to inform him that he could leave his post and move to safety. So the soldier remained and let the lava mud completely engulf him.

Some of us may doubt his wisdom in just waiting there, when no good could come of it. The desire to run must have been tremendous. But what we must all respect was the man's courage and self-discipline to remain at his post in the face of certain death.

READING:

Ephesians 6, 14–17. St. Paul's admiration for a Roman soldier provided him with an ideal illustration.

PRAYER:

Grant to us, Lord, this day to do whatever duty lies before us to be done, with cheerfulness and sincerity of heart. Help us in all things fearlessly to play the man. Remove from us all hypocrisy and pretence. Make us straight, unselfish, strong. So bring us to the ending of the day unashamed, and with a quiet mind. *Amen.*

The Lord's Prayer.

HYMNS: *Take up the cross, the Saviour said.*
Soldiers of Christ, arise.

35

SENSITIVE TO THE NEEDS OF OTHERS

Aim

To show that when we are sensitive to the needs of our fellow beings we grow spiritually.

Story

George, the local postman, was everyone's friend. He fetched groceries and chopped wood for the aged; he carried messages from one family to another; he listened to people's problems and gave them advice. He always seemed to have time for people and children loved him. Eventually George retired and, in due course, died.

Shortly afterwards, a very wealthy old lady who lived in a large house set in magnificent grounds, to whom George used to deliver letters, also died. At the Gates of Heaven she was met by St. Peter who asked her to follow him. They set off through the most beautiful countryside and passed many splendid houses set in delightful grounds. One house was particularly lovely, and the old lady commented on it.

'You know the man who lives in that house,' said Peter, 'it's old George the postman.'

'Well! Well!' exclaimed the old lady, 'he has been most fortunate. How did he come to be allotted such a lovely place?'

'He earned it,' replied Peter. 'Earned it!' she said in surprise. 'How could he possibly earn a place like that?'

'Well,' explained Peter, 'while George was down on earth, he sent us up a lot of material. For example, those trees and shrubs and pools represent all his kind works; those stones and bricks with which the house is built are his kind words; the furniture in the house represents his thoughts for others.'

'I see,' said the old lady, and settled back into her own thoughts.

Gradually they arrived in a large town and walked along a number of streets. The old lady couldn't help noticing that the quality of the housing was getting worse and worse as they progressed.

Eventually they entered a very dingy street and stopped outside a small and ill-kept house.

'Well, here we are,' said Peter, 'this is where you are to live.'

'But there must be some terrible mistake,' cried the old woman. 'I cannot possibly live in that hovel!'

'I'm sorry,' said Peter shrugging his shoulders, 'but that is all we could build with the material you sent up whilst you lived on earth.'

St. Matthew 6, 19–21. 'Do not store up for yourselves treasure on earth, where it grows rusty ... Store up treasure in heaven.'

PRAYER:

O Lord, give us more love, more self-denial, more likeness to thee. Teach us to sacrifice our comforts to others, and our likings for the sake of doing good. Make us kindly in thought, gentle in word, generous in deed. Teach us that it is better to give than to receive, better to forget ourselves than to put ourselves forward; better to minister than to be ministered unto. And unto thee, the God of love, be all glory and praise, both now and for everymore.

(Henry Alford, 1810–1871).

The Lord's Prayer.

HYMNS: *O thou not made with hands.*
O loving Lord, who art for ever seeking.

29.

SACRIFICE: I GAVE MY GOLD FOR IRON

Aim

When we give generously we find happiness and fulfilment.

Story

In the eighteenth century, Frederick the Great, King of Prussia, found himself surrounded by enemies. He had been involved in so many wars that he had completely emptied his treasury. Now he faced the greatest crisis of all. Unless he could find money to pay his army and purchase more arms, Prussia would be conquered and disgraced.

The King turned to his people and begged them to give him their gold and jewellery. He had nothing to offer them in return except poor copies of their necklaces, bracelets and rings made of iron. Many, though not all, answered his appeal and sufficient funds were raised to enable Frederick to conquer his foes.

Later, when prosperity had returned to Prussia, people began to dress again for state occasions and elaborate balls. Those people who had iron jewellery wore it in preference to gold, because it showed that the wearer had answered his country's call in a desperate hour. This iron jewellery became the highest status symbol anybody could wear because it declared to the world: 'I gave my gold for iron.'

READINGS:
St. Matthew 4, 18–22.
St. Mark 2, 14.
Five men leave security and follow Jesus.

PRAYER:
Teach us, good Lord, to serve thee as thou deservedst; to give and not to count the cost; to fight and not to heed the wounds; to toil and not to seek for rest; to labour and not to ask for any reward save the joy of knowing that we do thy will. *Amen.*

(Ignatius Loyola).

The Lord's Prayer.

HYMNS: *Jesus calls us! oe'r the tumult.*
For all the saints who from their labours rest.

30.

BEING ABOVE THE AVERAGE

Aim

To show that greatness can only be achieved by those who refuse to be just average.

Story

One of the myths of ancient Greece tells us of an inn-keeper named Procrustes who was famous for his bed. When an unsuspecting traveller booked in for the night, he was well entertained and then shown to his bedroom. In the middle hours of the night Procrustes would enter the bedroom and investigate whether the traveller fitted the bed or not. If he happened to be too short, he was securely strapped and stretched until he fitted the bed; if he was too long, then Procrustes chopped a piece off him until he was the right length. Either way, the traveller

38

died! Procrustes did not like people who were too short, nor did he like people who were too long.

Society is just like Procrustes! It, too, only likes average people. If a person is unsociable and lives below the average standard of society, every effort is made to stretch him to size, and probably this is a good thing. Unfortunately, however, society also has a tendency to dislike those who are above the average and puts pressure on them to conform.

It calls, therefore, for great determination and courage to refuse the ruling of the gang, or of our friends, and to stand for the principles which we consider to be right and true.

READING:

Ephesians 6, 10–13. '. . . then you will be able to stand your ground when things are at their worst. . .'

PRAYER:

O God we pray thee for courage to face unpopularity for the sake of truth; for courage to declare boldly our convictions, though they make us despised; for courage to break with evil custom and evil opinions. Give us strong hearts that will not fear what any person may do to us, or say about us. Give us, O Lord, the spirit of boldness, that being delivered from all fear of our fellows, we may be strong in thee, and very courageous. *Amen.*

(*J. S. Hoyland, adapted*).

The Lord's Prayer.

HYMNS: *Forth in thy name, O Lord I go.*
Fight the good fight with all thy might.

31.

HANDICAPPED LIVES

Aim

To show that with the right attitude a handicap can be turned to an advantage.

Story

One of the most famous violinists to grace the concert platform was the Norwegian, Ole Bull. Whilst giving a concert in Paris before an audience of keen music lovers, the 'A' string of his violin snapped. Ole Bull could justifiably have stopped and replaced the broken string, but the atmosphere would have been ruined. Instead he used his great skill and technique to complete the concert on three strings. The audience showed its deep appreciation of Ole Bull's performance by the number of curtain calls they made. He had turned a sudden handicap into a triumph!

Down through history we see handicaps resulting in splendid achievements. Beethoven wrote some of his greatest music after he had become deaf, and Milton produced great poetry after he became blind.

We all have some handicap or other to cope with. The important thing is to have a positive attitude towards it. If we react negatively, we become rebellious and full of self pity. Tackled correctly, a handicap can lift us to the great prizes of life. The Scandinavians have a saying: 'The north wind made the Vikings.'

It is inevitable that there will be hours when we will all hate our handicaps. Even Christ prayed that he might be spared the handicaps of the cross. But as it turned out in the end, no cross would have meant no Christ.

READINGS:
St. Mark 14, 32–42. 'Abba, Father, all things are possible to thee; take this cup away from me. . . .'
2 Corinthians 12, 7–10. Paul asks God to take away the thorn in his flesh.

PRAYER:
We remember before thee, O Lord, all who are handicapped through no fault of their own. Those who have lost their health and strength; the blind, the deaf, the dumb; those who suffer because of racial prejudice; those who have to cope with unhappy home backgrounds. Help them, we pray thee, in their difficulties and show them that there can never be a crown without a cross. *Amen.*

The Lord's Prayer.

HYMNS: *The head that once was crowned with thorns.*
From thee all skill and science fiow.

40

32.

TRANSFORMATION

Aim

When we invite God into our lives, He never seeks to change what we are but transforms us into what we have the potential to become.

Story

John Constable (1776–1837) was one of the greatest artists that England has ever produced, and is considered to be one of the greatest landscape painters in the history of art. Some of his best known paintings include *The Hay Wain, Dedham Vale, The Cornfield* and *Boat building near Flatford Mill*.

On one occasion, whilst at the height of his fame, Constable was on holiday. Staying at the same inn was an eleven-year-old girl who occupied much of her time painting.

It so happened that one afternoon the artist came across the young girl busily trying to paint a landscape scene but with very little success. He stood quietly by and watched her. He smiled as he saw her trying to make the paint behave itself and noticed that she was getting more and more exasperated.

The great man went and stood by her and asked her for her brush. The girl handed it over. With a few quick strokes, Constable, without in any way altering what the girl had done, transformed the painting into a thing of beauty.

READING:

St. Luke 19 vv 1–10. Zacchaeus is transformed into an honest tax-collector.

PRAYER:

Let your blessing, O Lord, rest upon our work this day. Teach us to seek after truth and help us to achieve it; but grant that as we increase in the knowledge of earthly things, we may grow in the knowledge of you, whom to know is life eternal; through Jesus Christ our Lord.

(Adapted from Thomas Arnold (1795–1842) Headmaster of Rugby).

(*Daily Prayer*).

The Lord's Prayer.

33.

TRUST IN GOD

Aim

When we learn to trust God, we shall be able to face any trial with complete confidence.

Story

On Christmas Day 1968 man first orbited the moon. It was a hazardous venture because of the many unforseeable difficulties which could suddenly and unpredictably occur. It called for enormous technical skill and brilliance from all those who designed, launched and tracked the space craft; and it demanded remarkable mental, physical and spiritual values from the three-man crew. One slight hitch or one miscalculation and the tiny space craft would have become a coffin for the crew members.

There was, however, one moment of high drama when the craft was four minutes late coming from the dark side of the moon. Everyone who was following the voyage on earth waited with bated breath, wondering whether something had gone wrong, because, whilst the craft was on the dark side of the moon, it was out of radio contact with earth. And then loud and clear came the voice of the navigator assuring Cape Kennedy that all was well. He went on to say that the crew wished to convey a Christmas message to all:

'In the beginning God created the heaven and earth. And the earth was without form, and void; and darkness was on the face of the deep. And the Spirit of God moved upon the face of the waters. And God said, Let there be light; and there was light. And God saw the light, that it was good: and God divided the light from the darkness.'

These men were men of faith. They had faith in the workmanship of their fellow men; faith in the mathematical calculations of their fellow physicists; faith in themselves; and above all faith in God.

Acts 27. Under the most appalling conditions of shipwreck, St. Paul's trust in God remained unshaken.

PRAYER:
Almighty and everlasting God, whose throne is eternity, and the farthest heavens thy dwelling place, yet who abidest in every faithful heart: Open our eyes we pray thee, that we thy children may know the things eternal to be our inheritance, and the lowliest place where thou art, to be our Father's house. *Amen.*

The Lord's Prayer.

HYMNS: *O Thou not made with hands.*
Eternal Ruler of the ceaseless round.

34.

WORSHIP

Aim

To show that an act of worship should be a moment of refreshment.

Story

A visitor to London a hundred years ago would have noticed that many men and boys earned their livelihood from carrying goods on their backs from one place to another. Sometimes the journeys would be quite lengthy and the carrier, or porter as he was called, would have to rest. If he were to put his burden on the ground, he would have to face the difficulty of lifting it back on to his shoulders again. So the porter was always on the look-out for a low wall or window-sill on which to place his burden at shoulder height. Some kind people actually erected suitable resting places round and about London. One such resting place still survives on the edge of a pavement near Green Park. It is quite simply made up of a wooden bar resting on two metal legs. Nearby an inscription reads:

> This porter's rest was erected in 1861 by the
> Vestry of Hanover Square, for the benefit of
> Porters and others carrying burdens.

43

The same sort of resting places are to be found in many of the large cities of India. There they are called Soomai Tangi which, simply translated, means 'a burden bearer'. These are made up of a stone slab placed across two uprights.

Some years ago when a new altar was placed in the Chapel of St. Christopher's College in Madras, the altar was made to represent a Soomai Tangi in order to remind all who worshipped there that worship should be a time of refreshment when we can come to God and rest our burdens on him awhile.

READING:

St. Matthew 11, 28. 'Come to me, all whose work is hard, whose load is heavy; and I will give you relief.'

PRAYER:

Set before our minds and hearts, O heavenly Father, the example of our Lord Jesus Christ, who, when he was upon earth, found his refreshment in doing the will of him that sent him, and in finishing his work. When many are coming and going, and there is little leisure, give us grace to remember him who knew neither impatience of spirit nor confusion of work, but in the midst of his labours held communion with thee, and even upon earth was still in heaven; where now he reigneth with thee and the Holy Spirit world without end. *Amen.*

(*Dean Vaughan* 1816–97).

The Lord's Prayer.

HYMNS: *Lord of all hopefulness, Lord of all joy.*
O God of Bethel, by whose hand.

35.

SEEING

Aim

If we really want to *see*, we must observe with care.

Story

Until about 1950 one of the most dreaded diseases to afflict young people in this country was Tuberculosis.

A doctor employed in the bacteriological laboratory of one of our hospitals tells the story that one of his tasks was to identify tuberculosis bacteria. A specimen was taken from a suspected person and carefully placed on a culture plate and left to grow for two or three days under a bell-jar. If tuberculosis was present, the bacterial growth could be observed under the microscope, and there was little hope for the victim.

On one occasion, the doctor, after having carefully prepared a specimen, forgot to cover it with the bell-jar. The plate lay exposed to the damp air over the weekend. When it was placed under the microscope and examined, it was found to be covered with mildew and the culture dead. He was rebuked by his chief and told to repeat the test. The spoilt plate was dropped into a waste bin.

Twenty years later, another doctor, Alexander Fleming, made the same mistake. But instead of throwing the spoilt plate away, he had a closer look at the mildew and the dead culture. He wondered whether there might be a connection between the two.

Further observations were made and various tests carried out. Eventually it was discovered that the mildew produced a substance which killed tuberculosis. This substance was given the name 'penicillin'; and has been responsible for almost wiping out tuberculosis as a killer disease.

The cure was there when the first doctor peered through his microscope at the dead culture, but he failed to see it. It took an Alexander Fleming to do that.

READINGS:
Acts 9, 1–19. Saul at last 'sees' that Jesus is the Son of God.
St. Matthew 5, 14–16. '. . . You are the light of the World.'

PRAYER:

O gracious and holy Father,
Give us wisdom to see thee,
intelligence to understand thee,
diligence to seek thee,
patience to wait for thee,
eyes to behold thee,
a heart to meditate upon thee,
and a life to proclaim thee;
through the power of the Spirit of
Jesus Christ our Lord. *Amen.*
(*St. Benedict*, 480–543).

The Lord's Prayer.

HYMNS: *All things bright and beautiful.*
Immortal, invisible, God only wise.

36.

BOASTING

Aim

To guard against being opinionated.

Story

Hundreds of miles out in the Atlantic there is a tiny island, so small that it is not to be found on any map. On this island there lived a frog all alone. There was no other form of life at all to keep him company.

Fortunately for the frog, a couple of migratory geese landed on the island once a year to rest awhile on their long journey. The frog looked forward with great anticipation to these visits, he enjoyed their company and loved listening to their descriptions of the different countries over which they flew.

'How I wish I could come with you,' he would often sigh. 'You have no idea what it is like being stranded here.'

The geese would sympathise with him and wish that there was something they could do to help, but there was nothing they could think of.

One morning after a particularly wild storm, the frog happened to be hopping along the narrow stretch of sand which skirted the island when he found a piece of string left behind by the tide.

As he looked at the string an idea began to take shape in his mind. He became very excited because the idea was so simple it just had to work. He carefully dragged the piece of string up to a safe place, and patiently settled down to await the arrival of the geese.

The weeks seemed to drag by, but at long last the geese arrived.

After the preliminary greetings were over, the frog outlined his plan to them:

'If each of you takes an end of this string in his beak, I can hold on to the middle part by my mouth and between you, you can carry me to the mainland.'

The geese examined the piece of string and agreed to give the plan a trial. After a few practice runs, the plan worked perfectly.

Eventually they left the island and headed into the wind. After many

46

hours flight, the mainland appeared in the distance and soon they were flying over fields and trees, valleys and hills. The frog was completely enchanted by the beauty of all that he saw.

The geese flew lower and lower so that the frog could have a closer view and they passed over people working in the fields and going about their tasks. When these people looked up and saw the amazing sight of two geese carrying a frog suspended between them, they could hardly believe their eyes.

'What a brilliant idea!' said one man.

'Who was the genius who thought out that method of carrying someone?' said another.

The frog, when he heard all this praise, couldn't resist the temptation of answering back. He pointed at himself and shouted, 'It was my idea! I am the genius who thought out the plan!'

But alas, when he opened his mouth, he plunged to his fate below.

READINGS:
St. Luke 18, 9–14. The parable of the Pharisee and the Publican.
St. Luke 14, 7–11. '. . . everyone who exalts himself will be humbled; and whoever humbles himself will be exalted.'

PRAYER Take from us, O God
All pride and vanity,
All boasting and forwardness;
And give us the true courage that shows itself by gentleness,
The true wisdom that shows itself by simplicity,
And the true power that shows itself by modesty;
Through Jesus Christ our Lord. *Amen.*
(*Charles Kingsley*, 1819–1875).

HYMNS: *Come down O Love Divine.*
Our blest Redeemer, ere he breathed.

37.

UNITY

Aim

To show that there is one God and Father of all, who is over all and through all and in all.

Story

Cornwall, Pembrokeshire and the west coast of Scotland have magnificent coast lines. There you will find large sweeping bays, tiny coves, narrow creeks and open estuaries reaching far inland. The variety of feature is breathtaking, each cove, each creek, each bay differs from the next. But notice one thing, it is the same tide that sweeps into all of them.

So it is with the religions of the world. They all differ in many respects; no two are the same. There is the religion of the Hindu, the Buddhist, the Muslim, the Jew and the Christian. Even within one religion there are marked differences. For example, within Christianity we find that there are Roman Catholics, Episcopalians, Presbyterians, Methodists, Pentecostals and Congregationalists. But it is the one Creator we all worship, it is the same God who flows through all.

READING:

St. John 10, 14–16. '. . . There will then be one flock, one shepherd.'

PRAYER:

O God, Father of all mankind, we think before thee this day of all thy children—
the people of Europe, with their rich treasures of the past, their knowledge and skill, and their great hope for the future—
the people of Asia, with their ageless wisdom and their great new ventures—
the people of Africa, with their warm hearts and their open minds, ready for a new destiny—
the people of America, with their life and vigour, their generous hearts, and their pioneering spirit—
and the people of Australasia, forward looking, strong and free.
O Lord, we praise thee for all the infinite variety of mankind. Teach us, by thy mercy, how we thy children can learn to live in unity, according to thy will. For Jesus' sake. *Amen.*

(*Senior Teacher's Assembly Book*).

The Lord's Prayer.

HYMNS: *All people that on earth do dwell.*
O worship the Lord in the beauty of holiness.

38.

THE LORD IS MY SHEPHERD

Aim

To show that through prayer and by letting God come into our lives, we get to know Jesus as a friend and guide.

Story

A number of friends held a party and invited many others to come along. As the evening progressed someone had an idea.

'Listen!' he said, 'It isn't often that we meet together like this. Let's have a concert!'

They all agreed and consented to take part. Some sang, some told funny stories, some recited poetry and one or two read passages from favourite books. One of the guests happened to be a well known Shakespearean actor, and when he stepped forward to make his contribution, everyone was surprised to hear him recite the Twenty-Third Psalm. He recited the psalm perfectly and everyone clapped their appreciation.

Sitting in the corner of the room was an old priest who was desperately hoping that he would not be called upon to perform. But one of the guests spotted him, and, pointing a finger in his direction, declared in a loud and humorous voice, 'Come on! You're next! We have all done our little bit, and you must do yours!'

'I'm much too old for that sort of thing,' said the priest, 'my voice has grown too shaky and my memory is very unreliable. Besides I am no good at telling stories and I cannot possibly sing.'

'But surely you know something!' they all chorused. 'You must know a psalm!'

'Well,' replied the priest, 'I do know a psalm, but it is the Twenty-Third, and that has already been recited.'

'It doesn't matter,' came the reply. 'We will hear it again; only this time from you.'

The old priest could see that there was no way out, so he very slowly got to his feet and clearing his throat began to recite the psalm.

They all listened in absolute silence as the old man repeated the well known verses. Eventually, when he reached the end, he turned and sat down. Still the silence remained. And then the room erupted. Everyone clapped and gathered around the priest to congratulate him. 'We've never heard anything quite like that,' said one. 'I have never been so moved,' said another. They all agreed that the old man had opened their understanding, so that they now saw for the first time what the writer of the psalm was trying to say.

Whilst all this was going on, the Shakespearean actor called for quietness and then, walking across to the priest, he said:

'I may know the Twenty-Third Psalm, but our friend here has an advantage over me, he knows the Shepherd.'

READING:

St. John 10, 14–18. 'I am the good shepherd; and I know my sheep and my sheep know me . . .'

PRAYER:

May the strength of God pilot us.
May the power of God preserve us.
May the wisdom of God instruct us.
May the hand of God protect us.
May the way of God direct us.
May the shield of God defend us.
May the host of God guard us against the snares of evil and the temptations of the World.
May Christ be with us, Christ before us,
Christ in us, Christ over us.
May thy salvation, O Lord, be always ours this day and evermore.

(*St. Patrick's Breastplate*).

The Lord's Prayer.

HYMNS:

The Lord's my Shepherd, I'll not want.
Father, lead me day by day.

39.

ACTIONS SPEAK LOUDER THAN WORDS

Aim

To show that what we are speaks for more than what we say.

Story

St. Francis of Assisi was famous for his wonderful preaching. One

50

day a young man, who wished to become a preacher, visited him and asked Francis if he could come on his next preaching tour, to watch the Saint in action. St. Francis readily agreed to the request.

Soon the Saint set out to preach in a nearby town and took the young man with him.

As they entered the town Francis began visiting many sick people in their homes. Frequently he stopped to talk with children and even joined in their games. Eventually, they reached the great square in the centre of the town, and Francis moved from stall to stall talking to the stall-holders, discussing the price of the produce, listening to their problems and offering them advice. Occasionally he helped peasants to unload their vegetables and gently soothed their tired donkeys.

The young man waited patiently, hoping that Francis would soon gather the crowds around him and start preaching to them, but Francis seemed more than content to move amongst people and chat.

Late in the afternoon Francis headed for home. The young man followed behind very disappointed. He had come all this way to study the ability of this great preacher, but so far he had not learnt a thing.

Unable to restrain himself any longer, the young man quickened his pace and caught up with the Saint and said:

'I thought you said you were going to preach today! And I don't mind telling you that I feel as though I have wasted my time.'

Francis smiled, and gently put his arm around the young man's shoulders and replied:

'But, my friend, I have been preaching! That's what it's all about. When I visit the sick, and play with children and mingle with the people on market day; when I give them comfort, and advice, and let them talk to me; when I give them a helping hand to unload and take an interest in their donkeys. That is when I am really preaching God's word.'

READING: Philippians 4, 8 & 9.

PRAYER:

Lord, make us instruments of thy peace.
Where there is hatred, let us sow love;
Where there is injury, pardon;
Where there is discord, union;
Where there is doubt, faith;
Where there is despair, hope;
Where there is darkness, light;
Where there is sadness, joy;

51

O Divine Master, grant that we may not so much seek to be consoled as to console; to be understood as to understand; to be loved, as to love; through the love of thy Son who died for us, Jesus Christ our Lord.

(St. Francis of Assisi, 1181–1266).

The Lord's Prayer.

HYMNS: *How sweet the name of Jesus sounds.*
God is working his purpose out as year succeeds to year.

40.

WORKING TOGETHER

Aim

Whatever our gifts, they are vital to the strategy of God.

Story

A visit to one of our great Cathedrals is an unforgettable experience. Its majesty and its soaring towers leave an indelible impression on the mind.

We can only stand and wonder at the genius of the architect who designed a building of such noble beauty.

But we must not forget the army of workers who enabled him to make his vision a reality. Those who quarried the rock and those who cut the stone to size and shape. Those who sawed the mighty beams which span the nave and those who carved the timber for the choir. Those who stained and cut the glass. Those who hammered and twisted metals into gates and screens.

Architects, treasurers, joiners, blacksmiths, masons, quarry-men, waggoners, scaffold erectors and labourers, all put their skills together, each dependent on the other, for the successful completion of such a mighty work.

READING:

1 Corinthians 12, 5–11. 'There are varieties of gifts, but the same Spirit...'

PRAYER:

Lord of infinite greatness, who hast ordered and adorned in equal perfection all that thou hast made; who hast set in glorious array the eternal heavens, and yet dost paint the lily that abideth but a day: Give us courage to attempt great things in thy Name, and equal faithfulness to do the small; to thy sole honour and glory, through Jesus Christ our Lord. *Amen.*

The Lord's Prayer.

HYMNS: *O loving Lord who art forever seeking.*
God of concrete, God of steel.

41.

LOVE

Aim

To show that nothing can resist the power of love.

Story

When it was decided to build a bridge across the River Hudson at New York, divers were sent down to explore the bed of the river. They discovered the wreck of a great sailing ship half-buried in the mud at a point where the engineers intended to sink one of the main piers. The wreck had to be moved. Tugs were summoned to the scene and attached steel ropes securely to the wreck. But to no avail, the wreck would not move.

Eventually somebody had an idea. At this point the River Hudson is tidal, that is, the sea level rises and falls twice every twenty-four hours. At low tide a number of large barges were towed out until they were floating above the wreck and were made fast to the ropes. Everyone waited. Gradually the barges began to rise on the incoming tide. Slowly and surely the old wreck was dragged up out of its muddy grave and eventually it was taken away. Nothing could resist the power of the rising water—which had the whole might of the Atlantic ocean behind it.

So it is with the love of God. Nothing can resist its power or conquer it.

1 Corinthians 13. The all embracing importance of love.

PRAYER:

Almighty God who gave us a new commandment that we should love one another: Give us also grace that we may fulfil it. Make us gentle, courteous and forbearing. Direct our lives so that we may look for the good of others in word and deed. And hallow all our friendships by the blessing of thy Spirit, for his sake who loved us and gave himself for us, Jesus Christ our Lord. *Amen.*

(*B. F. Westcott*).

The Lord's Prayer.

HYMNS: *Love divine, all loves excelling.*
Gracious Spirit, Holy Ghost.

42.

SACRIFICE

Aim

To show that man is never more noble than when he voluntarily submits himself to unselfish sacrifice.

Story

In 1665 when the plague was ravaging London, a parcel of clothing was sent to the village of Eyam in the Peak District of Derbyshire. Tragically it contained germs of the plague and soon twenty-three of the villagers fell victim to it.

Understandably, everyone in Eyam began to panic and families started to pack their belongings in order to leave before they too became infected.

At this point, the Vicar, William Mompesson, called the whole village to a meeting in the church. He pointed out to them that if they left they would in every probability carry the plague to all the surrounding counties, and many thousands would perish.

'I am asking you,' he said, 'to stay here; to isolate yourselves from the outside world, until the plague dies down.'

The villagers listened to the Vicar's advice and decided to stay. All approach roads to Eyam were closed, and large notices erected, warning would-be visitors that the village was under attack from the plague. Food was brought to agreed spots by surrounding neighbours, and the villagers settled down to their grim task.

Ten months went by and seventy deaths were recorded. At the end of twelve months two hundred and fifty nine people had fallen victim to the dread disease. A terrible toll for such a small community. But the plague was contained, and Eyam will always be remembered for its great sacrifice.

READING:

St. John 15, 11–17. 'There is no greater love than this, that a man should lay down his life for his friends.'

PRAYER:

O God our Father, who in the life of thy Son Jesus didst give to men the perfect example of thy love, accept and strengthen, we pray thee, the lives of those here who would follow him. Make us strong in will, brave in action, honest in faith: that by thy power our lives may show forth among men the beauty of his life, who is our brother and Lord, Jesus Christ. *Amen.*

The Lord's Prayer.

HYMNS: *Who would true valour see.*
Soldiers of Christ, arise.

43.

TELEMACHUS

Aim

However unimportant we may think we are, we can be sure that God has an important job in mind for us.

Story

The Colosseum in Rome has been described as the greatest theatre ever built on earth. Today it stands shattered and broken, but still it is one of the most impressive buildings in the world.

55

The kind of entertainment put on there for the citizens of Rome sixteen hundred years ago was the most bestial and horrible imaginable.

Wild beasts fought wild beasts; wild beasts fought men; and man fought man to the death, in what were called gladiatorial combats. The Romans gloated over all this blood-shed and in thousands came to witness these spectacles. Human life was cheap.

One day, as a gladiatorial fight was about to begin, a small frail old man got into the arena and stood between the two lines of advancing gladiators. He held his arms aloft and shouted:

'Hold, in the name of Christ.'

The gladiators stopped for a moment, not quite knowing what to make of the situation.

The spectators, however, were angry that anyone should have the nerve to interfere with their afternoon's sport. They began to shout:

'Kill him! Kill him! Get rid of him!'

The soldiers began to advance again. One brawny fellow stretched out an arm, grabbed the frail old man by the neck, and tossed him aside as though he were little more than a bundle of rags. But the old man struggled to his feet and thrust himself between the fast-closing gladiators. This time, however, one of them shrugged his shoulders impatiently and drove his sword deep into the old man. The frail body sank to the ground and a red pool of blood oozed into the sand of the arena floor.

A hush swept across the amphitheatre, everyone remained perfectly still. Then one of the spectators got up from his place and walked out. He was followed by another, and another, until the huge theatre was empty. Rome was disgusted with itself. And, of course, no one wanted to go to such a spectacle again.

It had taken an old, frail man called Telemachus to show the people of Rome that human life has dignity.

READING:

Acts 7, 54–60. Many believe that it was the way in which Stephen prayed for the forgiveness of his murderers that eventually led to the conversion of St. Paul.

PRAYER:

Teach us, O God,
to serve thee as thou deservest;
to give and not to count the cost;
to fight and not to heed the wounds;
to toil and not to seek for rest;

to labour and not to ask for any reward
save that of knowing that we do thy will;
through Jesus Christ our Lord. *Amen.*

The Lord's Prayer.

<small>HYMNS</small>: *When I survey the wondrous Cross.*
Lord of the Dance.

44.

COURTESY

Aim

Acts of courtesy are ways of showing our respect for one another and
are signs of our sensitivity towards our fellow beings.

Story

When King George V was Prince of Wales he paid a state visit to
Japan. As you might expect, the Japanese made the most elaborate and
careful preparations for such an important event. Everything was
planned down to the smallest detail.

The Prince arrived by ship and the quay-side was thronged with
thousands of spectators who had turned out to welcome him. A red
carpet had been laid from the docking point to the state coach in his
honour. As the Prince began his walk along the carpet, the crowd
became so excited that the police barrier burst and scores of people
spilled across the route.

The officials who were escorting the Prince hastily led him off in
another direction and instructed the coach to move on to a further
point. Then to their embarrassment, they noticed that lying directly
across their path lay a long shallow puddle of oily mud. Desperately
they looked around for something with which to cover it. There was
only one thing to hand and that was the Japanese flag. Without hesitat-
ing, one of the officials grabbed the flag and spread it across the middle
of the puddle so that the Prince might cross without soiling his shoes.

The Prince of Wales observed what had been done. He walked up
to the flag, saluted it, and then stepping to one side walked through
the puddle.

The act of courtesy had a profound effect on the watching Japanese, and from that moment the visit was a complete success.

READING:

St. Luke 7 vv 36–50. Jesus was too courteous to dismiss Mary Magdalene. Jesus reprimanded Simon the Pharisee for his lack of courtesy.

PRAYER:

Lord Jesus, make us this day courteous, considerate and kind one towards another, after your example towards all, for your Name's sake. *Amen.*

(Daily Prayer).

The Lord's Prayer.

HYMNS: *Forth in thy name, O Lord, I go.*
Pour down thy Spirit from above.

45.

CHRISTMAS I

Aim

There are many ways into the presence of Christ.

Story

The people present at the crib of Jesus:

Mary: She was chosen to be the mother of Jesus because she was pure. 'Blessed are the pure in heart for they shall see God.'

Joseph: He was there because he was chivalrous. He remained true and loyal to Mary. Never, at any time, did he leave her unprotected. Her welfare and comfort were his main concern.

Wise Men: They were present because they had used their intelligence. They had confidence in their observations and calculations and after a long determined search eventually found what they were looking for.

The Shepherds: When they were informed by the angels that Christ had been born, they were getting on with their job of shepherding.

58

Just ordinary men doing an ordinary job. It is in the routine work of life where nothing exciting ever seems to happen that God frequently reveals himself.

The Innkeeper: Many artists depict him as being present also. He was there because he felt sorry for someone in difficulty and tried to do something to help. It is no good just feeling sorry. We have got to do something about it.

READING: St. Luke 2, 1–20.
St. Matthew 2, 1–10.

PRAYER:

Almighty God, who hast given us thy only begotten Son to take our nature upon him, and as at this time to be born of a pure Virgin; Grant that we being reborn, and made thy children by adoption and grace, may daily be renewed by thy Holy Spirit; through the same our Lord Jesus Christ, who liveth and reigneth with Thee and the same Spirit, ever one God, world without end.

(Book of Common Prayer).

The Lord's Prayer.

HYMNS: *Girls and boys, leave your toys, make no noise.*
O little town of Bethlehem.

46.

CHRISTMAS II

Aim

To show that there are many ways of communicating our thoughts.

Story

A father appeared twenty-minutes early to pick up his daughter from a school party. Whilst he waited he stood quietly at the back of the hall and looked on with interest. He noticed that most of the young people were standing around in groups talking, whilst a few danced to what he considered an over-amplified record player.

The disc-jockey announced the next dance, and immediately everyone surged on to the floor and began to dance with tremendous enthusiasm. A complete transformation had come over the scene which did not go unnoticed by the father.

Later, on the way home, he asked his daughter why it was that a particular record could have such electrifying results.

'Because it's the top of the pops,' she replied.

'Really!' he exclaimed, 'but what is it that makes a record the "top of the pops"?'

'Its message of course,' she said, as though everyone should know.

'But,' said the father, 'no-one could possibly make out the words of the song being sung on that record; the music completely drowned them.'

'That doesn't matter,' she smiled, 'you don't have to use words to get a message across. You just let the music carry it into your mind.'

The father pondered on this statement for some time and realised that his young daughter was right. There are many different ways of conveying messages other than by words.

A painter when he wishes to communicate, uses his brush and paints.

A composer uses music.

A deaf man has to use sign-language.

A sailor will sometimes use flags.

A radio operator will use morse code.

When God wished to convey his message—his 'Word' so to speak—that he loved us, he sent it in the person of Jesus Christ his son.

READING:

St. John 1, 1–14. '. . . So the Word became flesh; he came to dwell among us, and we saw his glory . . .'

PRAYER:

Heavenly Father, who didst reveal thy love to mankind in the person of Jesus Christ. Grant that we may so study his teaching and follow his example that the love he came to show us may become rooted in our hearts, so that when men look at us they may see a reflection of thee. *Amen.*

The Lord's Prayer.

HYMNS: *Once in royal David's city.*
Hark! the herald angels sing.

47.

NEW YEAR

Aim

The one true guide we all have is God revealed in Jesus Christ.

Story

One of the loveliest and most majestic parts of Wales is Snowdonia; some of you may have been there on holiday.

Until recent times, visitors would never think of climbing Snowdon or exploring its neighbourhood without first employing a guide!

At the beginning of this century, a group of men arrived in the village of Betws-Y-Coed carrying coloured rods, tripods and chains, and spent many months surveying every part of the mountain range.

Not long afterwards there appeared on sale in the local Post Office for the price of sixpence, Ordnance Survey maps of Snowdonia, showing every track, landmark and peak.

On the first day of the maps' appearance, Griffith, one of the local guides, happened to be standing at his garden gate when he was hailed by a friend who lived near-by.

'I see you're out of a job!' he cried.

'What do you mean by that?' replied Griffith.

'Haven't you seen the maps on sale at the Post Office?' said the friend. 'They are so detailed even a little child could find his way around the mountains; and they only cost sixpence. People won't need your services any more, they'll just buy a map.'

'Is that so?' smiled Griffith. 'Tell me, friend, does the map show you what to do when a sudden fall of snow or a thick mist obliterates all landmarks and tracks?'

'No map can do that,' came the reply.

'There you are then,' grunted Griffith. 'Until they invent such a map, I shall still be required as a guide.'

READING:

St. John 14, 1–6. 'I am the way, the truth and the life.'
and/or

'And I said to the man who stood at the gate of the year: Give me a light that I might tread safely into the unknown. And he replied: Go out into the darkness and put your hand into the hand of God. That shall be to you better than light and safer than a known way.

(*M. Louise Haskins*).

Day by day, dear Lord of Thee
Three things we pray:
To see Thee more clearly;
To love Thee more dearly;
To follow Thee more nearly;
Day by day.

(*St. Richard of Chichester*).

The Lord's Prayer.

HYMNS: *Lord, behold us with Thy blessing.*
Father, lead me day by day.

48.

THE CRUCIFIXION

Aim

To explain the deeper meaning of the verb, to redeem; viz: to buy back something which originally belonged to you.

Story

Every summer John's parents took him on holiday to the sea-side. One year John decided that he would spend the long evenings during the winter constructing a model sailing ship. He saved up his pocket money, and with a little assistance from an aunt and uncle he eventually had the required amount to purchase the kit.

It was quite a ship to build, being over two feet long, and took many months to complete. His father helped him over one or two of the trickier problems and his mother advised him on the stitching of the sails, but basically, the end-product was John's work.

The big question now was, would it sail on the waves at the sea-side without capsizing?

The summer term gradually drew to its close and soon John and his parents were heading for the sea-side.

'At last,' thought John, holding the ship carefully on his knees, 'I shall be able to sail her under real conditions.'

By mid-afternoon they had booked into their hotel. John changed into his swimming trunks, and headed for the beach. He was delighted to find that the tide was in. He entered the water and, wading out up to his hips, carefully launched his ship. It floated perfectly! Imagine his excitement as he re-set the sails and re-adjusted the rudder to send her skimming in ever widening circles. The hours just flew by. And then it happened. A combination of current, a freshening breeze and an ebbing tide carried the ship away from him. He swam in pursuit as far as he dared and then turned back. He looked around for an adult who might go after it, but there was no-one within hailing distance. Helplessly he just stood and watched his ship floating further and further away until all hope seemed gone.

Blinking back his tears, John stumbled back over the shingle and headed for the hotel. There he told his parents what had happened. His father put his arm around his shoulders and said, 'Never mind I'll buy you another ship tomorrow.' But John just shook his head. He wanted the ship he had made.

Early the following morning John and his father walked the whole length of the beach in the hope that the tide would have brought the ship back in. But no luck! They repeated the walk in the afternoon, but again there was no sign of it.

Two days later passing one of those odd junk-shops which every sea-side resort seems to have, John noticed a sailing ship in its window. He paused, and had a closer look. He could hardly believe his eyes. It was his ship! On sale for £1.50p. As it happened the shop was closed for the afternoon.

Needless to say, the following morning John was standing on the shop door step with £1.50p. clutched tightly in his hand. Eventually the blind was raised and the door unlocked. Almost before the shop-keeper had time to get behind his counter, John had placed the money in front of him and asked for the boat in the window.

The boat was fetched and handed over. John held it carefully and examined it for possible damage, but to his relief it was in good shape. And then, holding it close to him he left the shop, murmuring to himself, 'You are mine! You are mine! You are doubly mine! I made you and now I have bought you!'

READING: St. Matthew 27, 33–50. The Crucifixion.

PRAYER:

Almighty God, we beseech thee graciously to behold this thy family, for which our Lord Jesus Christ was contented to be betrayed, and given up into the hands of wicked men, and to suffer death upon the

63

cross, who now liveth and reigneth with Thee and the Holy Spirit, ever one God, world without end. *Amen.*

The Lord's Prayer.

HYMNS: *There is a green hill far away.*
When I survey the wondrous cross.

49.

WHITSUN

Aim

God speaks to everyone in the language he can understand.

Story

Many years ago a Welsh girl came to London to serve as a maid in one of the big houses. On Sundays she travelled many miles across the city to worship with her own people in a Welsh church.

The people with whom she lived were very kind to her and invited her to come along with them to worship at the local church, to save her having to journey so far on her day off. But the girl very courteously refused, saying that she would rather make the journey to share in worship in the language which she knew and loved so well.

The master of the house smiled and very gently pointed out that Jesus was not a Welshman.

The girl understood what her employer was trying to say and quietly answered, 'I know that, Sir, but it is in Welsh that he speaks to me.'

READING:
Acts 2, 1–12. '. . . we hear them telling in our own tongues the great things God has done.'

PRAYER:
O God, who in the burning fire of thy love wast pleased to pour out the Holy Spirit on thy disciples: grant us by the same Spirit to be lit with heavenly desires and with the power to fulfil them; through Jesus Christ our Lord.

(*Book of Common Prayer*).

The Lord's Prayer.

50.

TRINITY

Aim

To show that belief in God the Father, God the Son, and God the Holy Ghost being one God need not be confusing.

Story

I am sure that you all know that the national emblem of Ireland is the shamrock. Let me tell you how this came to be.

St. Patrick was the Saint who carried Christianity to Ireland. Legend tells us that shortly after his arrival he succeeded in calling together a large number of fierce Irish chieftains to a meeting in a wood. There he spoke to them for three or four hours about Jesus Christ and the Christian faith.

When Patrick had finished speaking he invited the chiefs to ask questions.

One great bearded fellow got up and said:

'What I have heard here today has impressed me very much. I for one would like to accept this religion and make it my faith. But I cannot accept something I do not understand. We have heard references to God the Father, God the Son and God the Holy Ghost. Yet we are assured that there are not three Gods but one. Could the speaker explain how one can possibly be three or, if it comes to that, how can three possibly be one?'

Patrick felt every eye fixed on him and realised that this was a very critical moment. If he failed to give them a satisfactory answer now, he would never get as good an opportunity again.

Slowly he rose to his feet, and prayed for guidance. And there at his feet he noticed a shamrock. He bent down and carefully picked it and then holding it up he asked:

'What do I have in my hand?'

A shamrock,' they replied.

'How many shamrocks?' he asked.

65

'One,' they replied.
'How many leaves are there on a shamrock?' he asked.
'Three,' they replied.
'There we are then,' declared Patrick with a broad smile. 'I have shown you that three can be one and one can be three.'

The chiefs were convinced and accepted Christ into their lives there and then. And that is how the shamrock came to be the emblem of Ireland.

READING:
> St. Matthew 3, 13–17. . . . After baptism Jesus came up out of the water at once . . .; he saw the Spirit of God descending like a dove. . . .; and a voice from heaven was heard saying, 'This is my Son, my Beloved, on whom my favour rests.'

PRAYER:
> To God the Father, who first loved us, and made us accepted in the Beloved; to God the Son, who loved us, and washed us from our sins in his own blood; to God the Holy Ghost, who sheddeth the love of God abroad in our hearts: to the one true God be all love and all glory for time and for eternity.
>
> *(Thomas Kerr).*
>
> The Lord's Prayer.

HYMNS: *Three in One, and One in Three.*
Firmly I believe and truly.

ACKNOWLEDGEMENTS

Extracts herein used from *The Book of Common Prayer*, which is Crown Copyright, are used with permission; *A Book of Common Prayer for Schools* by permission of SCM Press Ltd; *Daily Prayer* (compiled by Eric Milner-White and G. W. Briggs) by permission of Oxford University Press; *Senior Teachers Assembly Book* published by Blandford Press Ltd; *Parish Prayers* (Frank Colquhoun) by permission of Hodder and Stoughton Ltd; The Dragon School Oxford for permission to use prayers from *Hymns and Prayers for Dragons*.